50 Plus Years of Pride: The Impact of
the Bars, Taverns and Clubs

D1446986

Michael Boyajian

Sal J. Calise, Editor

Jera Studios Publishing

50 Plus Years of Pride: The Impact of the Bars, Taverns and Clubs

Michael Boyajian

Sal J. Calise, Editor

ISBN: 9798623879912

Jera Studios Publishing

Cover design by Sal J. Calise

To Sal J. Calise, an inspiration.

Contents

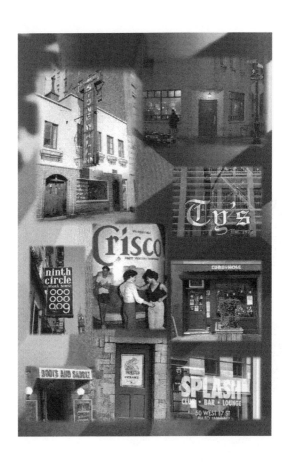

Preface

The 1980s were the best time to be in the bar business.   It was like the Roaring 20s.

I was blessed that I exited the business at the right time though. I knew enough was enough.

The bar industry can really burn you out especially since the 80s as I said earlier were like the 20s. In my mind I knew it was to time to exit and call it a day. If you can make decisions like that then you will go a long way in life, you will always be ahead.

Looking back at those days the only thing that kept me alive was days off going home to Brooklyn to a strong loving family. Every one of my business partners are dead today. This included one of my best friends and partner in the bars we owned. He did not know when to slow down.

One of the things I strived for was social networking, having friends in two different circles – no pun intended.

We were all disappointed in the bad rap the gay community had in the past. But that is changing now, disappearing little by little.

The reason why I feel that bars were important was because it gave people a place to socialize. Look at the success of Democratic or Republican political clubs that give people of like mind places to meet, socialize and network.

Because of this networking the gay community grew. The LGBTQ community went from being alienated in markets to now being in demand in those same markets.

Companies are spending millions of dollars to reach you so as to get your business while undoing the mistakes of the past knowing that you are now a "good commodity," using a term of business.

So again, the reason the bars were important was that it gave people a place to network and then expand that network to include friends and family.

This made you feel strong rather than alienated. A part of society rather than a hidden separate part of the world.

And this is why you have the protections under the law that we have today. And these laws will never change. Things will continue to grow positively for the gay community and everyone in fact because inclusion wins and exclusion loses.

Looking back on the late 70s and the 80s you can see the times have changed today. People used to disguise themselves or use different names if they held high positions. It was like a crime to go to a gay bar to the extent that you would have different entrances to your bar.

We came a long way because of strong support from friends and family. People out there today know they are not alone.

The perfect example is Michael Boyajian the author of this book and a co-author of the marriage equality book, The People's Victory. Michael and his wife Jeri were activists for the gay rights movement for many years like many other straight people who we must thank for their support. I could list hundreds of supporters but let me just end by saying thank you to Michael for writing this book.

Sal J. Calise, June 2020

Inclusion wins, exclusion loses.

14

Introduction

"I sing the body electric," --Walt Whitman, Leaves of Grass

"I saw the best minds of my generation destroyed by madness, starving hysterical naked" -- Allen Ginsberg, Howl

36 hours of viewing Allen Ginsberg tapes on YouTube and I felt I was ready to face the task of writing this book. Here it goes.

Today is not the climax of 50 years of pride since Stonewall. Today is the day we all go together through a new door into the future.

There have been some low points like the AIDs crisis but there have also been some high points like marriage equality. Yet through it all the LGBTQ community had shown great resilience. Our testimonials support this viewpoint.

And as for the bars, they were not places to get drunk but to seek shelter from intolerance and find acceptance and comradery like in the TV show Cheers.

I hope we at nycpride2019 met your expectations, thank you for your support and here is a toast to the next 50 years and to Sal J Calise whose idea created that Facebook page and this book.   Peace.

Sincerely, Mike Boyajian, June 2020

1 – Sal J. Calise

Sal J Calise remembers being secretive as a young man but he discovered a world of friendship in the gay bars. It was more than drinking, there was comradery. They were like a social club or something out of Cheers.

Sal's mother and aunt were always very supportive. His mother and aunt always told Salvatore whatever makes you happy in your life makes us happy it's your life and you need to live it. Sal's mother and her sisters were beacons of support.

His father was very upset when he found out Sal was gay. But Sal's uncle told the father either accept him or lose him for good. And that's what the bars were about they were places of acceptance.

Sal Calise's story begins in 1976 when he first encountered a gay bar, the 9th Circle. He became friends with the bartender Tree who now is in his 80s and works at Stonewall Thursday through Saturday noon to 8:00.

His next bar was Julius' which would eventually be owned by Sal's friend Freddy Lux. People would walk in and say you are in my seat, like in Cheers the

regulars had their permanent seats.
The bar also has a dead corner where
they had photos of some of their dead
customers.

Things were bad for gays back then.
Once in 1978 a group of firemen on the
job on a FDNY truck, pulled over and
beat up gays for holding hands. Today
the FDNY and its commissioner march in
the Pride Parade.

Then in the 1980's the AIDs crisis hit the
community. Hundreds were dying.
Victims would go into the hospital and
never come out. There were so many
colorful characters and Sal says despite

21

the AIDs crisis it was the height of the gay era. Yes, you would go into a bar and find out this one was gone and this one too. He used to admire a group of five older men when he was in his 20s. They would take turns eating at each other's houses, so you would only have to cook one meal a week. But that got all wiped out by AIDs. Only one of the five survived.

But still they were golden years with all the bars, discos and new wave clubs. When the gay pride parade started out it was just about a 5 block long street fair. When Sal had a club in Brooklyn no one would come in the main entrance only through a discrete side street entrance but today you don't have to do

that you can have the entrance on
Seventh Avenue and the crowds will
come in.

The people who came out were the real
heroes. And even today in the Bible belt
people are accepting because a well-
loved family member would be gay, and
they wouldn't want to lose that person.
Sal says, going into the 2020
presidential. Let's end the hate.
"Inclusion wins, exclusion loses"

2 – Andrew Miller

Andrew Miller says things have changed greatly since he was a kid and being gay meant something dirty and being hidden.   Andrew works for the City of New York and things today are not entirely perfect. He works with runaway kids who are mostly LGBTQ and thrown out of their homes many times for religious reasons. Andrew has yet to find anything like that in Jesus's teachings.

But still the LGBTQ community has emerged from the shadows gaining equal rights with straights so that they are today full human beings. This is supported by the libertarian view of staying out of people's lives. Andrew says in the past being gay meant being a confirmed bachelor. When is the last time you heard that term?

Andrew agrees that LGBTQ travel overseas is like African Americans in the 1960s traveling in the United States when a green book was needed. He also feels that past homophobic political rhetoric may have had the unexpected effect of igniting the LGBTQ base.

3 – Anna Cognetto

Anna Cognetto says the fight for equality brought her into the LGBTQ movement starting in 1977. Back then many people were still in the closet. Anna was in college writing letters to elected officials asking for visibility and acknowledgement of the LGBTQ community.

Anna says many good things have happened since more and more people came out of the closet including marriage equality and the revocation of Don't Ask Don't Tell. It has even helped when it came to businesses and the government flying the Pride flag.

Anna was unofficially married by a Unitarian minister in New Paltz as part of mayor Jason West's operation. Later Anna became ecstatic when she learned New York had passed marriage equality. It did not surprise her that New York State under the leadership of Governor Andrew Cuomo had legalized marriage equality.

But she says the fight is not over and she is ready to roll up her sleeves and continue to fight for equality.

4 – Eileen Petvold

Eileen Petvold started going to Fire Island with her husband Paul in 1974. They went there for the dancing. They loved to dance and danced at every bar in Cherry Grove. Eileen says dancing made many friendships that last to this day.

Paul passed away in 2017 and Johny Pool and others told him don't worry she will be safe here. And she has been and is now buying a unit in what she calls paradise.

She talked about how Johny ran the Bar Ball where entertainers and workers were recognized with awards for their achievements to the profession. It was held every year at the old Copacabana and then a few other places ending at the new Copacabana where it ended five years ago after a 48 year run.

The AIDs crisis devastated the island. Everyone was in a panic, fear was on everyone's faces. Nobody knew what was going on. But things settled down. Things have changed from when she first started going to the island, some good some not so good but you get used to it all.

5 – Scott Weiser

Scott Weiser has known he was gay since he was 12 years old and so did his sister who used to kid him. He had girlfriends but only to distract the attention of straights who were not LGBTQ friendly. He has been bullied but someone had always had his back including his husband David.

Scott has been in a wheelchair since birth. He has a master's in social work and specializes in social security disability issues.

He was on the MENY Board and was a MENY liaison to his state senator. He and David run Rainbow POD which is an LGBTQ activity group. They host pool parties and bowling events. He hopes to march in this year's pride parade.

6 – Robert Lassegue-Reyes

Robert Lassegue-Reyes got involved with LGBTQ advocacy when the gay softball team he was on got thrown out of a straight league. His team turned around and started a gay sports league.

From there Rob was brought into MENY where he was involved from start to finish. He was in disbelief when he got the call that the New York State Senate had passed the marriage equality bill. They were told it might pass but we're surprised nonetheless.

In 2013 Rob decided to step away from activism. He is now the general manager at the Ice Palace on Fire Island where he rubs elbows with famous entertainers, drag queens and movers and shakers like Johny Pool.

He has to miss the Pride Celebration this month because the entire Ice Palace staff is going and he has to watch the fort. C'est la vie.

7 – Michael Sabatino and Robert Voorheis

Michael Sabatino and his husband Robert Voorheis first got involved with the LGBTQ movement when they met with a financial planner and realized they did not have the same protections as married couples. This led them to getting involved with MENY which had just gotten started.

Michael and Robert were married in Canada and the Westchester County Executive recognized their marriage. Unfortunately the mayor was sued over this. But in 2009 the New York Court of

Appeals ruled their marriage valid. So technically they became the first married same sex couple in the state.

When Michael was asked how he felt about the triumph of marriage equality he says frankly he never thought it would happen in their lifetime.

Today Michael is the first openly gay elected official in Yonkers and Robert is actively involved with Yonkers Pride. Yonkers has an outstanding Human Rights Campaign LGBTQ rating and the mayor has an LGBTQ advisory committee.

8 – Brian Silva

Brian Silva was brought into the LGBTQ movement when his uncle died from AIDs. It opened up his awareness to the power of advocacy.

After that he was in New York during the Prop 8 campaign doing remote phone banking. Prop 8 passed but Brian met people from the marriage equality movement in New York. He volunteered and one thing led to another and he became the leader of MENY. Then when marriage equality passed in New York and MENY transitioned into MEUSA he led the new organization.

Everyone than realized that marriage does mean full equality and NEAT was formed led by Brian. NEAT works on multiple LGBTQ issues using phone banks. Their greatest accomplishment was passing the Trans gender rights bill in Massachusetts through the legislature and then successfully defending against an opposition ballot measure.

Brian recalls a funny story when he was canvassing for an LGBTQ issue in Maryland. He went into a person's house thinking it was going to be a big

argument but in the house he saw it
was two women and their child and
they said you don't have to convince us
and they all laughed.

Brian helped create the book by over 50
authors that chronicles marriage
equality, The People's Victory.

42

9 – Cathy Marino-Thomas

Cathy Marino-Thomas first knew there was a problem out there when she and her partner at the time were denied housing time and again. They then had an encounter with a guy yelling slurs and throwing bottles at them. They had to really push the police to make an arrest but in the end he did spend time in jail.

Cathy then realized you could not legally recreate the power of a marriage license. So she went to a Marriage Equality New York meeting. 6 people were there and they had 8 for their first march and they were soundly booed. At one protest they were up against 5000 haters. The police had to place Cathy and her 14 fellow protestors in barricades for their own protection.

But in less than 20 years they leveled the marriage equality playing field in New York by vote and nationwide by a Supreme Court ruling.   Now when they march they have 300 people and they are cheered.

Cathy retired from activism until June 12 2015 when a gunman slaughtered 49

LGBTQ people so today she works with Gays Against Guns. Their first meeting was booked for 60 people and 300 showed up.

10 – Dave Warren

Dave Warren was a Republican and in the closet up until the 1990s. He was asked to be the Young Republicans for Reagan chair but turned it down fearing embarrassment for himself and the campaign if outed.

His mom asked him his orientation and when he told her she had a meltdown but she was educated and did research and told Dave it was ok to be gay.

And in the 1990s the New York Republican party was gay friendly led by the Brooklyn GOP, the state Young Republicans and Congressman Bill Greene who was a "beam of light." But than when John Ravitz gave his concession speech and thanked Dave and the Log Cabin gay Republicans the gays were booed at the liberal Metropolitan Republican club. Dave says it was because wealthy out of towners had pushed out the liberal native New Yorkers.

Dave left the GOP because of the Iraq War and Bush's push for a constitutional amendment outlawing marriage equality. Dave felt the amendment was intrusive.

Dave is now an active Democrat and
past president of his local Democratic
club and a bike advocate. He says W
and Trump are the "Dark Ages" of gay
rights and President Obama was "bright
sunshine."

Dave works for the FDNY and the
department especially under
Commissioner Nigro is pro LGBTQ. In
fact the FDNY marches proudly in the
Pride Parade.

11 – Johny Pool

LGBTQ bar scene celebrity Johny Pool tells the story of the rise of Cherry Grove on Fire Island beginning with his work as a lifeguard to his standing as the blender king.

Cherry Grove in the 1960s was an international destination for gays even though police boats raided the bars there regularly. Bars included the Beach Hotel and Club visited by celebrities like Grace Jones.

Things got wild in the 1970s when Johny got tired of running drinks from the bar to the pool. So they set up a mini bar for him by the pool. He and his friends were getting high one day when they got the idea to make a blender drink using peaches, liquor and juice. Well one thing led to another and Johny became the blender king with 32 blenders turning out drinks.

The HIV crisis in the 1980s changed everything but things are back on the party track again.

Johny, who worked at Stonewall, says the gay community has come a long way

whereas today it's an alternative

lifestyle that accepts all other lifestyles.

12 – Johny Pool

Johny Pool was on his way to Fire Island when the protests broke out at the Stonewall in 1969. Johny is a noted figure in New York and at Cherry Grove. Now he has over 115,000 Twitter followers.

He recalls the gay bar scene back in the day. You had to stand facing the bar or risk arrest and if there were three or more gays talking on a street corner you spent the night in jail.

But oh did they have some great bars. Johny reports that the gay bar scene started on the Upper Eastside than moved to the mid Eastside and then the lower Eastside. From there it moved to the Upper Westside and then to the Village.

There was of course Stonewall and Julius'. But there was also Ty's, Oh Johnnys, the Cubby Hole, the Duplex Piano Bar, Don't Tell Momma's, Waverly Waverly, the Ninth Circle, Roses Turn, New Jimmy's and more.

Pool was in drag as Cher at Oh Johnnys once when Sue Simmons and Joan Rivers came in along with her dog and he went up to her and said I don't always look like this and Joan laughed. The bar was big with theater people.

13 – Tom Bernardin

Tom Bernardin is the unofficial historian for an historic gay bar, Julius' in Greenwich Village. The bar had a gay rights protest there three years before the one at the Stonewall.

In 1966 a Ukrainian society bar refused to serve gays. The law at that time prohibited serving gays because they were "unruly."

 A number of people decided to have a sip in protest at Julius'. When they ordered a drink the bartender placed his hand over their cup and refused to serve them.   The group decided to sue the liquor authority and turned to the New York City Human Rights Commission. The authority realized it was fighting a losing battle and dropped the restriction. It was a great moment in the gay rights community.

This all led to the question today of with all the gay rights today do we still need gay bars. Tom says yes just like you need African American churches. It's a place to bond with your community and be a member of that community.

14 - Margaretville

There is a buzz out there about a new LGBTQ summer Mecca rising in LGBTQ friendly Margaretville in the Western Catskills joining other hot spots like P-Town and Fire Island as well as straight summer getaways like the rest of the Catskills, the Berkshires, the Hamptons, Beacon and Litchfield.

My wife Jeri and I had a summer home in Margaretville and have fond memories of our summers there. We were up in the Catskills for a wedding at the Onteoro Mountain House and the day before went house hunting. Price

led us to Margaretville a place we had
never been to before even though we
had been visiting the Catskills since
childhood.

When you entered Margaretville there
was a real estate office with a large
window filled with listings with photos
of the homes. One jumped right out at
us and the agent took us to the home.
It was on the side of a mountain
overlooking another mountain. We
went into the bedroom and they had
ceiling to floor windows overlooking the
forested mountainside. It filled the
room with green light.

We fell in love with the house and Jeri said this is the one I want. We lived in Brooklyn Heights and wanted to get into the real estate market and the best way was through a weekend home. We put a bid on the house and by the time of the wedding we had signed a binder. We moved in just a few months after that and the partying began.

We were never big entertainers but now we had guests up every weekend. Friends and family alike. When Jeri's family rolled in which was just about every other weekend we had like 20 people sleeping in the small cabin. Different groups of friends would come in at different times. There was Sal Calise and his crew, Rick, Kevin and

Dave. Scott and Eileen and their daughter. Long Islanders Jack, Alice, Bill and Hanna and many others.

Some people would be driving through the Hudson Valley and would call and ask to overnight and we would say yes of course just bring in a case of beer. Canadian Molson's Ale and Martinis shaken not stirred were the drinks of choice. Real old school.

We would inevitably end up at one of the restaurants on Main Street and party there until closing. One place had a summer camping style game center out back with pool tables, fooz ball and ping pong. Again old school.

After the restaurants closed it was back
to the house to party till dawn and wake
up with hot coffee on the front lawn
watching the colorful songbirds at the
feeders with mist rising on the distant
mountain. Then breakfast at the Round
Barn food market. We would barbecue
for lunch.

Every Saturday night the Bellayre Ski
Center had a concert. We saw everyone
from Ray Charles to Dr. John there.
Only we had lawn seats outside the tent
and could only see the performers' feet.
But above us were the bright stars and
even the Milky Way. Picnic baskets and
white wine were the items of choice for
a night out at Bellayre.

There was also a great deal of flea markets and ample fishing and hiking opportunities. I landed my first trout fly fishing here and smoked trout was sold everywhere. A nice day trip from Margaretville was to Cooperstown to the Baseball Hall of Fame and the Farmers Museum and much more.

There was also a nice bookstore nearby called the Bibliobarn and yes it was an old barn. The couple who owned this place were relocating their bookshop from Virginia to Massachusetts when they stopped in the Western Catskills, fell in love with the area and opened their store here. Naturalist John Burroughs' home was also nearby.

In the winter there was downhill and cross country skiing at Bellayre as well as snow shoeing. We had to sell the house when we moved out of our studio apartment and into a home in the Hudson Valley. We had not been back in ten years but I went up this spring and at one point a golden eagle flew parallel to our car as if to say we miss you Mike and Jeri.

15 – Cathy Marino-Thomas

Cathy Marino-Thomas met her wife Sheila in Provincetown after Cathy had a bad break up. They immediately became friends and their relationship took off out of the P-Town party world. Soon they decided they wanted a child and Cathy under went three years of insemination. Finally on the night of a big party she took her pregnancy test a day early and came running out of the bathroom yelling I am positive. She had a beautiful pregnancy and gave birth to Jackie near winter.

When Jackie was two years old Sheila and Cathy returned to P-Town with their baby to spend uninterrupted time with her in a place that held fond memories for the two. They wanted Jackie to be part of those memories from the get go. Now when they go up they bring Jackie and her friends and their dog. Jackie by the way is in her second year now in college in Philadelphia and already living off campus. This author remembers Jackie as a child at the marriage equality events running around with a black and white cookie saying these are my two moms.

Jackie brought their family closer together by bringing in Sheila's mom who had been resistant to the relationship. They said this is your grandchild now do you want to be a grandmother. Her answer was an unequivocal yes and they became a very tight family with Sheila's parents and Cathy's mom who is the family cheerleader.

Cathy was at the forefront of the marriage equality movement but once that came to a successful end she moved on to the gun issue becoming a member since inception of Gays Against Guns or GAG if you will. Now Cathy says with marriage equality her opponents were armed with bibles now with GAG her opponents are armed with guns.

16 – Rick Kanar

Rick Kanar says it was awful growing up in Western Pennsylvania as a gay teenager. He came out when he was thirteen and found that he was not accepted. Then he met a group of gay teens who saved his life and he felt acceptance for the first time. He and his friends would go up into the mountains of coal country and get high and just dream of a better future.

Then like Jack Kerouac Rick hit the road after high school and hitchhiked down to Ft. Lauderdale where he worked in restaurants and bars. He partied heavily here and spent a lot of time in Key

West.   People were much more accepting here than in coal country.

He did a brief sojourn partying up in Albany NY but soon headed south again to Lauderdale. Rick was an outpatient in rehab when he met his lifelong friend Sal Calise.   The next thing you know Rick is heading north again only this time to Brooklyn USA with Sal the party king of New York City. Rick was headed to Bensonhurst to be specific.

It was here that he began attending parties hosted by the likes of Governor George Pataki and Senator Roy Goodman and finding that these politicians were accepting of him. The

next thing you know he is running up
and down the state doing political
campaigns but only for nice politicians.

After many years Rick returned home to
family in Pittsburgh where rent was
cheaper and where people were now
very accepting and Rick is now very
comfortable with himself and has no
problems wearing purple shoes and a
man purse because even in coal country
things have changed for the better for
the LGBTQ community.

17 – Michael Fisher

Film maker Michael Fisher has created a gem of a movie with his work entitled Cherry Grove Stories.   The film captures the spirit and history of the LGBTQ party enclave on New York's Fire Island community of Cherry Grove.

He interviewed scores of people who tell us about the struggle the gay community initially faced and their triumph in the end as we learn of the famous bars like the Ice Palace, the Sea Shack and the Monster from Fire Island celebrities of all ages including Johny Pool.

Michael first learned this history of Cherry Grove from the late Michael D'Alosio who told him of how it all started out with about thirty people who first said let's have dress up parties that eventually led to total drag on Saturdays and then every day.

These were tough times though. The police arrested them frequently for lewdness in public, published the arrest in the local papers and that resulted in the loss of their jobs. Things were so bad that the residents had to hide their attire beneath their floors that could only be reached by trap doors. Well things have changed today with everyone coming out of the closet and public acceptance.

Michael has been on Fire Island since 1985. He came to New York in the late Seventies. He loves both Cherry Grove and New York. So he and many others love the fact that Cherry Grove is a short drive or train ride from Manhattan.

Michael got together with some other people and came up with forty questions to ask forty people about Cherry Grove for the movie and that is the key to the film's success and broad appeal at all the film festivals around the world.

The movie is available on Amazon, ITunes, YouTube and even at Target stores. The film is distributed by Breaking Glass Pictures.

18 – Matt Alexander

Matt Alexander is the mayor of Wappingers Falls, NY. His greatest accomplishment as mayor has been the revitalization of the village in the scenic Hudson River Valley. Mayor Alexander is originally from L.A. or Lower Alabama if you will, Mobile to be exact. He ended up in the Hudson Valley because his dad was at West Point.

Matt was in finance and antiques in addition to being mayor.   He has a popular antiques store in the area. He was not involved with the LGBT movement per se because he was 15 in

1981 at the height of the AIDs calamity and he was scared to death of dying so activism was the last thing on his mind.

However he did lobby his local state senator personally, Stephen Saland, and his work and that of others led to Senator Saland casting the deciding vote in the Marriage Equality legalization bill in New York State. Matt says that he and his partner, Tony, of 23 years did not realize the importance of marriage equality until it became legal and that his discussions with Saland were very personal to him.

Matt's favorite getaway is Provincetown and he has been going there for thirty years now. His favorite bars are the Triangle and the Maverick. These are all fun places but they are also sanctuaries for Matt, a getaway from a once hostile world.

Mayor Alexander's mantra in politics is what have you done lately and for Matt the answer is quite a lot.

19 – Francena Amparo

Dutchess County Legislator Francena
Amparo identified as an LGBTQ person
in High School. She experienced
resistance at home and at school.
Today though her family is on board or
at least neutral but for her father who
does not want to talk about it. There is
a lack of communication and
acknowledgement between her and her
father especially now that Francena is
engaged to her partner Marissa.

In her youth she sought sanctuary at the
Hendrick Martin Institute which no
longer exists. She also found sanctuary

at the Loft in White Plains and the LGBTQ Center in Manhattan. She did have a favorite bar which was Henrietta's around Christopher and Hudson.

She found many Gay Friendly places using online guides back at the inception of the internet like Purple Roof and Planet Out. Today her enjoyment comes from serving her constituents and helping out wherever help is needed.

20 – Rae Leiner

Social justice activist Rae Leiner had an awkward time growing up in the 1980s and 90s because she did not know immediately what being gay was or where to go to be with others like herself. It caused a great deal of conflict which she diffused through internal actions.

For instance she would draw cartoons with a man and a women and in reality she would be the man and the woman would be someone she had a crush on. Sometimes men would want to date her but ultimately the fact that she was gay would force her to break away from that person. She had to overcome a dominant heterosexual society while coming to terms with her own place in the LGBTQ community.

Many sought sanctuary in bars and vacation places but Rae took a different way and that was through academics in her alternative high school in Spanish Harlem and in a small liberal arts college where she found people like herself.

She also had another level of conflict which was her "blackness." She was biracial with an over protective Jewish father and a black mother. So she had the conflict of moving between black

and white worlds on top of everything
else.

There were even in her academic
sanctuary problems with the
heterosexual world where for instance
during a travel semester she had a child
with a male. Just before she was to give
birth she realized that she could not
have a male female relationship so she
went back to campus.

She ended up living with a gay man who
had a child and they had a mutual
friend. The mutual friend pressured Rae
to avoid gay relationships. Which
created a great deal of conflict until one
time when the friend was a way and Rae

got sick and needed help getting her child to the start of school some gay friends came in and helped her get the child to school and pick up the details of what she needed to know about the schooling until she got better.

Her friend returned and got mad about the gay friends and took off.   In the end it turns out that this friend was herself gay and undergoing some sort of conflict. As for Rae, having found solace in school, and at the Metropolitan Museum of Art and her career which was social activism specifically environmental justice and prisoner rights and that is where she is today.

21 - Fredd E. Tree

Here are some of the names on the committee for the Bar Ball which was a celebration and awards ceremony that bound the Gay Community together.

The original members of the committee included: Johny Pool, Johnny Savoy,

Sal Maggio, Frank Rampino, Ed O'Hara, Clara O'Hara, Chuck Dima, Lou Prince, and Cathy Hogan.

The committee later expanded to include: Tree, Jim Bozart, and Kelly.

When the Bar Ball first started, it was always a Monday. Monday because most older bartenders where off on Monday and so were hairdressers.

We would meet at a certain bar for a few hours, then all the bars that wanted the event the next month put their name in a hat and thats who got the event the next time.

We also had bus trips for a few days to Atlantic City, Asbury Park and Fire Island.

One year we held a black-tie dinner dance at the Copacabana. The first Copa on East 60th St. The original Copa. Then they moved to West 57th Street, then closed for a few years. Then they reopened on West 34th Street, and they ended up on West 46 Street the old China club.

At first we had the Jerry Scott Trio performing with various singers in the lounge. The Lavender Orchestra performed in the main room. After a few years we had Celeste do the music.

Johny and I have put 40 years into the Bar Ball being in the end the only two involved with tickets. After that we called it quits.

Besides bartending I wrote for many LGBTQ newspapers and magazines. There was Michaels Thing, Knight Magazine, Next, Parlee, Greenwich Village Press and others.

I was 30 years old the day of the Stonewall riots and I'm still working there at 81 years young.

Then there was the 9th Circle. I started at the 9th Circle in the early 70s. I started as a doorman to help my friend have a few days off, just two days. After a short time the owner and manager said they want to try me out as a bartender. I told him I don't drink and I never made a drink, the owner said you'll learn to do both. I worked at it for 25 years until the owner died. His son ran it into the ground and it closed.

Some of my customers were Rock Hudson, Peter Allen, Lou Reed, Harvey Fierstein and so many more.

Some people said it was a bar for people to hustle, It happened on occasions. It was a family for the people that were there all the time and they were my family. I hear from people all the time that they miss that bar. Yes, drugs were sold there but in those days most people did them. The owner Bobby was a carney man. He owned games of chance in Coney Island and was owner of Under bar's.

9th Circle was a famous steakhouse, the ninth circle of hell, Dante's inferno. On the wall was a picture of Dante's inferno and an autographed photo of Janis Joplin who was a friend of the owner. I do miss that place, after that I started working at Julius the oldest bar in the city. For my 81 years I've had a great life I look forward to my future

22 – Helen Buford

Helen is the current owner of Julius'
leasing the space from a corporation
Helen and her late husband Eugene ran
the bar together. Helen took over after
Eugene's death. Before Helen and her
family Julius' was run by Freddie Lux.

Julius' is the one of the oldest LGBTQ
bars in New York opening in 1890. Prior
to that and beginning in 1864 it had
served the public as a grocery store.

Julius' started to attract a gay clientele
in the early 1960s. It was the site of one
of the earliest pre Stonewall gay rights

protests. It was a sit in known as the sip in.

At that time it was illegal to serve gays alcohol and for gays to even speak to one another in a bar.

They were able to talk to one another by talking into a long mirror behind the bar that way they did not face each other in violation of the law.

The April 21, 1966 sip in was organized by the Mattachine Society and was in response to draconian State Liquor Authority laws against gays.

NYCLGBTSITES.ORG according to Ken
Lustbader documents all LGBT historic
sites and events like Julius' and their sip
in. They helped to get Julius' on the
National Register of Historic Places.

Ken and his colleagues at the historic
project, Andrew S. Dolkort, Jay
Schockley and Amanda Davis, have
gotten state and national recognition
for many LGBT historic sites and events.

The bars alone include just to name a
few, Julius', Stonewall, Beach Haven
Bar, Black Rabbit, Bum Bum Bar, Crazy
Nanny's, Cubby Hole, Pandora's Box,
Fifth Avenue Bar, Friends Tavern, Jackie
60, Kooky's, Mayfair Bar, Meow Mix,

Tony Pastor's Downtown, Love Boat, Mad Hatter, Uncle Charlies, Paradise Garage, Park Villa II, Pfaff's, Portofino, Ramrod, San Remo Café, Sea Colony, Slide, Snake Pit, Starlite Lounge, Studio 54, Swing Rendezvous, Tenth of Always and The Saint.

Getting back to Julius' and the sip in, it emulated the sit ins being carried out at that time in the 1960s in the South by the Civil Rights movement.

The Mattachine Society publicized the plight of gays by the use of public photographs documenting the crushing discrimination they were suffering from in the bar scene which was the only sanctuary available to the gay community at that time prior to social media.

The bar celebrates the fight for the gay community to be served alcoholic beverages by holding a celebration of the sip in every third Thursday of the month and calling it Mattachine night.

The Mattachine Society was an early LGBT civil rights group. They fought for LGBT rights long before it became a popular issue. They brought light to the community in the dark early days prior to Stonewall.

April 21, 2016 marked the 50th Anniversary of the famed empowering sip in. The bar was at one time a speakeasy during Prohibition and was known as the Nine Doors.

It was illegal to break a police padlock on the door to a bar during Prohibition so the owners would build a new door bypassing the lock out. Eventually they had nine doors and hence the name the Nine Doors.

The bar did not get its first liquor license until 1934 and Helen has the original license. There is a portrait painting of one of the speakeasy owners whose

104

name was Texas Guinan.   She may have been the girlfriend of a previous owner.

THE 40TH ANNUAL BAR PEOPLE'S BALL
THE COPACABANA
268 WEST 47TH STREET OFF OF 8TH AVE., NYC
On Monday Oct. 12, 2015 7pm - 12am
Celeste At the Piano - Dinner & Dance With D.J. George

Join us as we give a salute
To all passed honorees
With a special salute to
The Stonewall Inn
where pride began
As well as Tree
bartendering
for over 45 years

2015 will be the last
year it's hosted by
Uncle Johny Pool

Special guest performance
by Shaquita

Ticket Includes Cocktail Hour 7 to 8
Dinner Dance 8pm - 12am
Open Bar 7pm - 12am
Tickets $160.00
BLACK TIE IS OPTIONAL

TICKETS MUST BE PURCHASED BY SEP. 26.
TICKETS ARE NON-REFUNDABLE.

Re-opened in 1993

In 1969

About the Author

Michael Boyajian is a retired attorney and former human rights judge. He has written 30 books. He was one of the key members of Marriage Equality New York and he was a co-author of The People's Victory. He lives in the Hudson Valley with his wife Jeri and their three cats where they enjoy their garden and library.

Made in the USA
Middletown, DE
13 June 2020